greatest
artists

Claude Monet

Michelle Lomberg

www.av2books.com

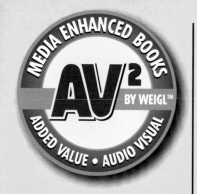

AV² provides enriched content that supplements and complements this book. Weigl's AV² books strive to create inspired learning and engage young minds in a total learning experience.

Your AV² Media Enhanced books come alive with...

Audio
Listen to sections of the book read aloud.

Key Words
Study vocabulary, and complete a matching word activity.

Video
Watch informative video clips.

Quizzes
Test your knowledge.

Embedded Weblinks
Gain additional information for research.

Slide Show
View images and captions, and prepare a presentation.

Try This!
Complete activities and hands-on experiments.

... and much, much more!

Go to **www.av2books.com**, and enter this book's unique code.

BOOK CODE

H 5 5 9 6 3 9

AV² by Weigl brings you media enhanced books that support active learning.

Published by AV² by Weigl
350 5ᵗʰ Avenue, 59ᵗʰ Floor
New York, NY 10118
Website: www.av2books.com

Library of Congress Cataloging-in-Publication Data

Names: Lomberg, Michelle, author.
Title: Claude Monet / Michelle Lomberg.
Description: New York : AV2 by Weigl, 2016. | Series: Greatest artists | Includes index.
Identifiers: LCCN 2016004400 (print) | LCCN 2016005068 (ebook) | ISBN 9781489646194 (hard cover : alk. paper) | ISBN 9781489650313 (soft cover : alk. paper) | ISBN 9781489646200 (Multi-user ebk.)
Subjects: LCSH: Monet, Claude, 1840-1926--Juvenile literature. | Painters--France--Biography--Juvenile literature.
Classification: LCC ND553.M7 L66 2016 (print) | LCC ND553.M7 (ebook) | DDC 759.4--dc23
LC record available at http://lccn.loc.gov/2016004400

Printed in the United States of America in Brainerd, Minnesota
1 2 3 4 5 6 7 8 9 0 20 19 18 17 16

032016
210316

Editor: Heather Kissock   Art Director: Terry Paulhus

Every reasonable effort has been made to trace ownership and to obtain permission to reprint copyright material. The publishers would be pleased to have any errors or omissions brought to their attention so that they may be corrected in subsequent printings.

Weigl acknowledges Getty Images, Corbis, Alamy, and iStock as its primary image suppliers for this title.

CONTENTS

AV² Book Code.. 2

Meet Claude Monet... 4

Early Life.. 6

Growing Up.. 8

Learning the Craft... 10

Early Achievements.. 12

Master Class 14

Major Works 16

Timeline of Claude Monet 20

Path to Success.. 22

Claude Monet's Legacy 24

On Display... 26

Write a Biography.. 28

Test Yourself 29

Artistic Terms 30

Key Words/Index... 31

Log on to www.av2books.com........................ 32

Meet
Claude Monet

Claude Monet is considered one of the most influential artists of all time. His Impressionist style paved the way for more abstract forms of art.

Woman with a Parasol

Claude Monet's art is known for its misty landscapes and dreamy garden scenes. Looking at his tranquil paintings, it is difficult to imagine the artist as a rule breaker who shocked the art world. Monet broke tradition by moving his easel from the studio to the outdoors. He used vivid colors and quick, loose brushstrokes to paint the world around him. In doing so, Monet helped found an artistic movement that changed art forever.

Monet worked to capture the essence of a moment in his paintings. Details were suggested, not shown.

Monet is best known as one of the key founders of **Impressionism**. Since the 17th century, painting in France had been influenced by the Academy of Fine Arts. The Academy frowned on the use of bright colors, visible brushstrokes, and everyday subject matter. Impressionist painters turned their backs on these standards. To them, using bright colors and visible brushstrokes was a way to show the effects of light and color on their subjects. Painting everyday subject matter let them showcase the world in which they lived.

Monet's career spanned more than 65 years. In that time, he created more than 2,500 paintings and drawings. His ideas about painting influenced other artists of his time, as well as many of the artists that followed.

Art lovers continue to be fascinated by Monet's works. Displays of his paintings draw crowds even today.

Early Life

Oscar-Claude Monet was born in Paris, France, in 1840. His father, Claude-Adolphe Monet, was a grocer who had plans for Claude to take over the family business. Claude's mother, Louise-Justine Aubrée Monet, was a singer. Claude had one older brother, Léon. When Claude was five years old, the family moved to Le Havre, a bustling port in northern France.

Claude went to a private school until he was 11 years old. He then transferred to a local school for the arts. There, he studied Latin, Greek, drawing, and other subjects. Even though the school day was only four hours long, Claude preferred to spend his days outdoors, wandering along the coast instead of sitting in a classroom.

Le Havre sits on the coast of the English Channel at the mouth of the Seine River. It is France's second-largest port, after Marseille.

When he was in class, Claude filled his notebooks with doodles. As a teenager, he drew **caricatures** of his teachers and sold them in a local shop. These drawings earned the disapproval of Claude's father.

In 1857, Claude's mother died. Claude left school and went to live with his aunt, Marie-Jeanne Lecadre, a widow with no children of her own. Unlike Claude's father, Lecadre supported young Claude's artistic ambitions. Claude remained with her in Le Havre until 1859, when he moved to Paris.

"I didn't become an Impressionist. As long as I can remember, I always have been one."

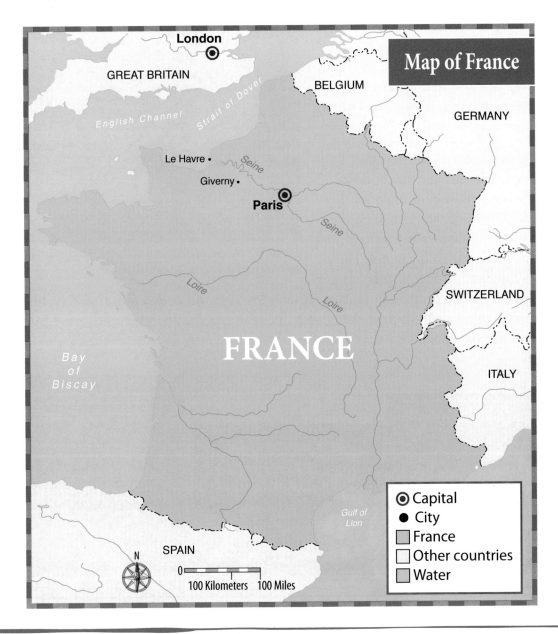

Map of France

Legend:
- ◉ Capital
- ● City
- ☐ France
- ☐ Other countries
- ☐ Water

Growing Up

Monet's caricatures were early evidence of his great talent. They were so popular that they led to a demand for portraits as well. Monet sold his pictures in the shop of Monsieur Gravier, a framer and **stationer**. Gravier thought that Monet could learn a great deal from Eugène Boudin, a painter of landscapes and seascapes. When the two artists were in his shop one day, Gravier introduced them.

At first, Monet resisted the idea of learning from Boudin. He did not like Boudin's work. Boudin, however, had seen the younger man's drawings and was impressed with his talent. He introduced Monet to plein air, or outdoor, sketching and painting. Monet loved it and decided to make art his career. Although Monet's father was not enthusiastic, he reluctantly gave his son permission.

Claude's first caricatures were of his schoolteachers. Their popularity led to requests for drawings of local townspeople.

Monet's parents called him Oscar in his youth, not Claude.

Monet sold his caricatures for 10 to 20 francs each.

Monet's father offered to get his son out of military service if he agreed to give up art. Monet refused.

Monet used the money he had earned from his caricatures to move to Paris in 1859. Once there, he began attending the Académie Suisse. This school provided models for artists to draw and paint, but did not offer formal lessons.

In 1861, Monet was **drafted** into the French army. He was posted to Algeria, where he was supposed to serve for seven years. When Monet fell ill after only one year, his aunt came to his aid. Lecadre offered to pay for Monet's release from service on the condition that he take formal art lessons. Monet returned to France and began to study at the studio of Charles Gleyre, a Swiss painter.

At the Académie Suisse, Monet met the artist Camille Pissarro, who would become a fellow Impressionist.

Monet was a soldier with the Zouaves during his time in Africa. The Zouaves were a French infantry unit known for their flamboyant uniforms.

Before they were known as Impressionists, Monet and his associates were called the Batignolles Group, after the area in Paris where most of them lived.

Learning the Craft

Monet studied in Gleyre's Paris studio from 1862 to 1863. Gleyre was a traditional painter. He taught his students to study and draw artworks from past eras. While his teaching had little influence on Monet's style, it was at Gleyre's studio that Monet met other artists who shared his views on art. Monet, along with Pierre-Auguste Renoir, Frédéric Bazille, and Alfred Sisley, would form the core of the early Impressionist movement.

While Monet studied under Gleyre, he was also learning from fellow plein air artist, Johan Barthold Jongkind. Jongkind was trained in the Dutch landscape tradition. This style favored dark colors and careful compositions. However, it was Jongkind's interest in light and his spontaneous technique that appealed to Monet. He felt that Jongkind completed the education that Boudin had started. Monet acknowledged Jongkind as his true artistic master.

Even though Jongkind's paintings are classical in style, they are known for their focus on light and atmosphere, features that would become an important part of the Impressionist style.

Monet also turned to the artists of the Barbizon school for inspiration. This group of landscape painters often met in the Forest of Fontainebleau, near Paris. The artists based their works on their own sensations and experiences. Their art challenged the traditional views of the time. In 1863, Monet began to paint in the Forest of Fontainebleau, too. His works from this period show the loose brushwork and **dappled** light that were to define his future style.

One of Monet's best-known paintings from the Forest of Fontainebleau is *The Bodmer Oak*, which he painted in 1865.

If Monet did not like something he had painted, he painted another picture over it.

Monet would often paint an entire work, from start to finish, outdoors.

Not only did Monet like to paint garden scenes, he was also a master gardener.

Early Achievements

In the 1860s, the Paris Salon could make or break an artist's career. At this annual event, a jury from the Academy of Fine Arts selected works of art for a grand **exhibition**. Thousands of works were displayed, and thousands more were rejected. **Art dealers**, collectors, and **curators** attended. If they liked what they saw, they often made deals to show and sell an artist's works. In 1865, the jury accepted two of Monet's seascapes. This was a great honor for the 25-year-old artist.

"It's on the strength of observation and reflection that one finds a way. So, we must dig and delve unceasingly."

Monet's success continued in the years that followed. In 1866, the jury accepted one of his landscapes and a portrait of a model named Camille Doncieux. Another seascape was accepted in 1868. Later that same year, Monet also won a silver medal at an exhibition in Le Havre.

Monet married Camille Doncieux in 1870. She continued to model for him until her death in 1879.

After Monet's initial successes at the Salon, juries began to reject his work. The Academy was a conservative organization. It saw Monet's work as too **avant-garde** for the Salon. Monet and other artists from the Gleyre studio decided to host their own exhibitions. Calling themselves the Société Anonyme des Artistes, Peintres, Sculpteurs, Graveurs, etc., these artists held a group exhibition in 1874.

Monet contributed a harbor scene to this first exhibition. Called *Impression, Sunrise,* it is a loosely sketched oil painting of the port in Le Havre. After seeing it, a writer made fun of the painting in a magazine, playing on the word "impression." Others began to call the Société Anonyme artists Impressionists. The artists soon adopted this name for themselves.

The Paris Salons were held in the Musée du Louvre until the mid-1800s. They were called salons after the Salon Carré, the hall in which they were held.

Master Class

Claude Monet is known above all as an outdoor painter. Working en plein air gave him valuable insights about light and shadow, and prompted him to develop new painting techniques to represent them. New developments in the manufacturing and storage of paint made Monet's outdoor work easier, and influenced his choice of colors.

Claude Monet and His Wife in His Floating Studio by Édouard Manet

En plein air

Plein air painting was Monet's passion, and he went to great lengths to make it possible. One of the ways he did this was by designing and building equipment that made outdoor painting easier. For one painting, he dug a trench for an 8-foot-tall (2.4-meter) canvas so that he could reach the top of it. He then devised an easel with a pulley system to raise and lower the canvas. Monet even adapted a boat to create a floating studio. He could often be seen painting in it as he drifted along the Seine.

Shadows and Light

More than anything, Impressionists were fascinated by light. Monet developed new painting techniques to emphasize the effects of light as it shone through trees and on water. While earlier artists carefully blended paints, Monet used pure colors. Instead of smooth, invisible brushstrokes, Monet worked with short dabs of paint. His use of the visible brushstroke, or tache, was revolutionary.

Shadows also fascinated Monet. Working in studios, earlier artists had used blacks and grays to paint shadows. Painting en plein air, Monet saw that shadows cast by sunlight could be purple and blue.

In Monceau Park

A New Kind of Color

Monet and his fellow Impressionists used blues and purples extensively in their works. This move away from the warm earth tones that had been popular in recent years was supported by a range of new **synthetic** paints that became available in the 1800s. These paints were made from chemicals rather than natural pigments. While the colors between the two types of paint were similar, synthetic paints produced more vibrant shades. As a result, Monet was able to build his **palettes** with new, brighter colors, such as cobalt blue, cerulean, ultramarine, and manganese violet.

Water Lilies

Portable Paints

While synthetic pigments made the Impressionist palette possible, it was the paint tube that enabled plein air painting. The tin paint tube with a screw cap was invented by the American artist John G. Rand in 1841. Before they had paint tubes, artists carried oil paints in pig bladders tied with string. The bladders had several downfalls. They could not be fully resealed, allowed paints to dry out, and were prone to bursting. Lightweight, portable paint tubes allowed Monet the freedom to complete his paintings outdoors.

Cliff Walk at Pourville

Major Works

Besides his paintings, Monet created numerous drawings and **pastels**. Most of these works depicted the immediate world around him, whether he was in his garden at home or experiencing the bustle of Paris.

Women in the Garden

To modern eyes, this painting is a tranquil outdoor scene. In 1866, however, it challenged conventional ideas about art. The canvas measures 8.4 feet by 6.7 feet (2.6 meters x 2.0 m), roughly the size of a garage door. At the time, paintings of such a large scale were usually reserved for historical subjects. Here, Monet depicts a commonplace moment in time.

In this painting, four women gather by a tree along a garden path. Bright patches of sunlight shine through the trees. These patches cast cool shadows on the women's elaborate dresses.

DATE: 1866 **MEDIUM:** Oil on canvas **SIZE:** 100 x 80 inches (254 x 203 centimeters)

Impression, Sunrise

Completed in 1872, *Impression, Sunrise* features sketch-like brushwork, a limited palette, and a lack of detail. All of this works to give the painting an unfinished look. Sharing his experience, or impression, was more important to Monet than creating an accurate representation of reality.

The painting shows watercraft and harbor structures in **silhouette** against the morning sky. The Sun is a bright orange circle shining through blue mist. Its reflection is portrayed by a line of loose orange brushstrokes on the blue water. Blue, which dominates the painting, remained an integral part of Monet's palette throughout his career.

DATE: 1872 **MEDIUM:** Oil on canvas **SIZE:** 18.9 x 24.8 inches (48 x 63 cm)

Boulevard des Capucines

Monet showed *Boulevard des Capucines* at the first Impressionist exhibition, in 1874. The scene was painted from the very room in which the exhibition was held—the former studio of the photographer Nadar. In this painting, Monet shares the photographer's eye for striking cityscapes from unusual vantage points.

This painting looks down onto a busy Paris street. A line of bare trees divides the lower half of the canvas diagonally. To the left, carriages hurry away from the viewer. To the right, darkly clad pedestrians bustle along the broad boulevard. On the right edge of the painting, two men in top hats watch from a balcony.

DATE: 1872 to 1873 **MEDIUM:** Oil on canvas **SIZE:** 31.6 x 23.75 inches (80.3 x 60.3 cm)

Coquelicots [Poppy Field]

In 1871, Monet and his family moved to Argenteuil, a picturesque village on the Seine not far from Paris. It was here that he painted one of his best-known works. *Coquelicots [Poppy Field]* showcases the artist's mastery of color and composition. This painting was also shown at the 1874 Impressionist exhibition.

Four figures stroll through a field of poppies under a cloud-dappled blue sky. The poppies are rendered as two-tone dabs of red. A row of dark trees marks the horizon line. The figures are virtually faceless, but nonetheless crucial to the composition, their path suggesting a diagonal line from the center left to the bottom right of the canvas.

DATE: 1873 **MEDIUM:** Oil on canvas **SIZE:** 19.7 x 25.6 inches (50 x 65 cm)

Timeline of Claude Monet

1840

Oscar-Claude Monet is born in Paris, France, to Claude-Adolphe and Louise-Justine Aubrée Monet. Claude-Adolphe owns a neighborhood grocery store. Louise-Justine is a singer.

1856

After meeting Monet in a local stationery store, artist Eugène Boudin introduces the younger man to plein air painting.

1862

Monet studies in the Paris studio of Charles Gleyre, where he meets Renoir, Sisley, and other future Impressionists.

1870

Monet marries his model, Camille Doncieux. When the **Franco-Prussian War** devastates Paris, the couple seeks refuge in London.

1872

Monet paints *Impression, Sunrise* for an upcoming exhibition. The work inspires the term Impressionism.

1883

Monet moves to Giverny, a village in northern France. Here, he designs and develops the garden that will inspire many of his future paintings.

1892

Twelve years after Camille Doncieux's death, Monet marries Alice Hoschedé, a widow with six children.

1926

Monet dies of lung cancer in Giverny, France, at the age of 86.

Path to Success

In July 1870, the Franco-Prussian War began. By mid-September that year, Paris was surrounded by German troops. Monet and Camille Doncieux, now his wife, fled to London, England. There, Monet met Paul Durand-Ruel, a French art dealer. Durand-Ruel agreed to help Monet with his career. He bought Monet's works, showed them in London, and offered the painter a room in his house to use as a studio. He also began to promote Monet's paintings to people in the United States. Durand-Ruel believed that Impressionist art would sell well there.

While working on *Water Lilies*, Monet's eyesight was threatened by cataracts, and he lost his ability to distinguish colors. He read the labels on his paint tubes to remember what the colors looked like.

Like many artists, Monet sometimes faced financial problems. However, with Durand-Ruel's support, he prospered. Over time, Monet was able to buy a house in the French village of Giverny. Here, he began to develop the garden that would become his outdoor studio. The garden featured numerous flower beds, but its highlight was the water garden. Planted with lilies, reeds, irises, and willows, it became the inspiration for many of Monet's best-loved paintings.

In 1889, Monet began painting what was to become his first major series. Based on some haystacks behind his house, the paintings show the haystacks at different times of day and in different seasons. Other series soon followed, featuring subjects ranging from a medieval cathedral to Monet's own water lilies—a series made up of about 250 paintings. The series format allowed Monet to explore his greatest interest, the ways in which light changes a viewer's perception of a subject.

The water lilies series culminated in a project unprecedented in scope. To celebrate the end of World War I in 1918, Monet offered to donate a grand work to France. Called *Water Lilies*, the work is made up of eight panels that cover an area of more than 2,000 square feet (186 square meters). Monet took 10 years to complete it. The paintings now hang in two rooms in the Musée de l'Orangerie in Paris.

The Creative Process

Artists are creative people. They have vivid imaginations and are able to think in abstract ways. Still, in order to create, they must have a process, or series of steps to follow. While most artists will adapt the process to suit their individual needs, there are basic steps that all artists use to plan and create their works.

Gathering Ideas
Observing and taking inspiration from surroundings

Researching
Studying the subject or topic to determine the approach

Forming Intent
Deciding on a subject or topic to explore

Planning the Work
Obtaining the materials needed to create the work

Outlining the Project
Sketching or developing a model to follow

Creating the Work
Applying the previous stages to the creation of the final product

Making Revisions
Changing elements that are not working

Requesting Feedback
Asking for opinions from others

Completing the Work

Claude Monet's Legacy

Monet died on December 5, 1926, at the age of 86. He had spent his last years painting scenes from his water garden, even though his eyesight was failing. His stepdaughter Blanche Hoschedé, the daughter of his second wife, cared for him in his old age. Monet was buried in the Giverny cemetery. His funeral was small, attended only by family and close friends.

Monet and his stepdaughter shared a love of art. As a teenager, Blanche was both his assistant and student. She later became an artist in her own right.

Monet's son Michel inherited the property at Giverny, and Blanche Hoschedé cared for it until her death in 1947. When Michel died in 1966, his will stated that the property should be given to the Academy of Fine Arts. By that time, the garden and buildings had fallen into disrepair. Restoring the house and gardens was a 10-year project. Today, visitors to Giverny can see Monet's house and gardens much as they were when he lived and painted there.

Monet's house features two main gardens. In front of the house is a flower garden. The water garden is accessed through an underground passage.

Monet's paintings remain popular with art lovers all over the world. People continue to flock to galleries to see the artist's works. Today's art collectors have been known to pay extremely high prices for an original Monet. *Nymphéas*, a painting of water lilies, sold for $54 million in 2014. *Water Lily Pond* sold for $80.5 million in 2008, the highest-priced Monet painting to date.

The gift shop at Monet's Giverny home has a wide selection of items featuring his artworks, ranging from shopping bags to tea towels.

People can own Monet's art in other ways as well. Many of his best-known works have been used to create commercial products. Monet's paintings have been reproduced on notecards, calendars, plates, and coffee mugs. These items are sold in gift shops around the world.

Monet's water lily paintings continue to be popular. In 2015, another *Nymphéas* painting sold for more than $33.8 million.

On Display

onet's works are held in public and private collections around the world. Visitors to major art galleries and art museums can see them displayed along with works by other Impressionists.

Musée Marmottan Monet

Paris's Musée Marmottan Monet holds the world's largest collection of Monet paintings. Many of these works came from Monet's son Michel, who bequeathed his personal collection to the museum in 1966. The Marmottan's collection has grown even larger with gifts from private collectors and donors. Housed in a former hunting lodge, the building became a public museum in 1934. Originally exhibiting paintings from the early 1800s, the Marmottan began acquiring Impressionist paintings in 1957. When the museum received the 1966 donation, a new gallery was built specifically for Monet's works.

The Musée Marmottan Monet is home to 100 of Monet's paintings.

Art Institute of Chicago

Thanks to Durand-Ruel's quest to find American buyers for Monet's paintings, many of the artist's works are held in American collections. The Art Institute of Chicago has many pieces by Monet, including some of the caricatures that he drew as a youth. Founded in 1879, the institute moved to its current location in central Chicago in 1893. The institute

The Art Institute of Chicago houses one of the largest permanent collections in the United States.

has undergone several expansions over the years. Its collection of more than 300,000 works of art is now housed within eight buildings. The institute has approximately 45 Monet works in its collection.

National Gallery

The National Gallery, in London, England, was founded in 1824 by the British government. Its initial collection was housed in the home of an art collector. The gallery moved to its current location in central London in 1838. Today, the National Gallery's main focus is Western art, with a particular interest in works from the 13th to 20th centuries. It has dedicated one of its exhibit rooms to Impressionist works, featuring art by Manet, Pissarro, Sisley, and Monet. Here, visitors can view several of Monet's landscapes, seascapes, and snow scenes alongside works by his **contemporaries**.

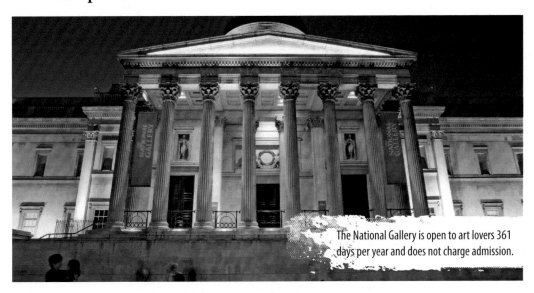

The National Gallery is open to art lovers 361 days per year and does not charge admission.

Write a Biography

All of the parts of a biography work together to tell the story of a person's life. Find out how these elements come together by writing a biography. Begin by choosing a person whose story fascinates you. You will have to research the person's life by using library books and reliable websites. You can also email the person or write him or her a letter. The person might agree to answer your questions directly.

Use the chart below to guide you in writing the biography. Answer each of the questions listed using the information you have gathered. Each heading in the chart will form an important part of the person's story.

Parts of a Biography

Early Life
Where and when was the person born?
What is known about the person's family and friends?
Did the person grow up in unusual circumstances?

Growing Up
Who had the most influence on the person?
Did he or she receive assistance from others?
Did the person have a positive attitude?

Developing Skills
What was the person's education?
What was the person's first job or work experience?
What obstacles did the person overcome?

Early Achievements
What was the person's most important early success?
What processes does this person use in his or her work?
Which of the person's traits were most helpful in his or her work?

Leaving a Legacy
Has the person received awards or recognition for accomplishments?
What is the person's life's work?
How have the person's accomplishments served others?

Test Yourself

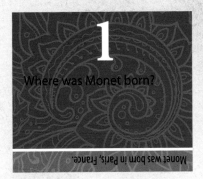

1
Where was Monet born?

Monet was born in Paris, France.

2
For which kind of art did young Monet first become known?

Monet was known for creating caricatures in his youth.

3
Which artist introduced Monet to plein air painting?

Eugène Boudin introduced Monet to plein air painting.

4
Which Dutch painter did Monet consider his true artistic master?

Monet considered Johan Barthold Jongkind his true artistic master.

5
What was the name of the model who became Monet's wife?

Camille Doncieux was the model who became Monet's wife.

6
In what year did the Paris Salon first accept paintings by Monet?

The Paris Salon accepted its first Monet paintings in 1865.

7
Which painting gave the Impressionists their name?

The Impressionists were named after Monet's painting *Impression, Sunrise.*

8
Who was Paul Durand-Ruel?

Paul Durand-Ruel was an art dealer who supported Monet's career.

9
Where did Monet plant his water garden?

Monet planted his water garden at his home in Giverny, France.

10
What work did Monet dedicate to France after World War I?

Monet dedicated *Water Lilies* to France after World War I.

Artistic Terms

The study and practice of art comes with its own language. Understanding some common art terms will allow you to discuss your ideas about art.

abstract: based on ideas rather than reality

brushwork: the way an artist applies paint with a brush

canvas: cotton or linen cloth used as a surface for painting

ceramics: articles made from clay that has been hardened by heat

composition: the arrangement of the individual elements within a work of art so that they make a unified whole

easel: a folding stand used to hold up a painting while the artist is working

engraving: a print made from an image cut into wood or metal

etching: prints made from images drawn with acid-resistant material on a metal plate

form: the shape or structure of an object

gallery: a place where paintings and other works of art are exhibited and sometimes sold

medium: the materials used to create a work of art

mood: the state of mind or emotion a painting evokes

movement: a stylistic trend followed by a group of artists

permanent collection: a collection of art owned by a museum or gallery

perspective: a technique used by artists to show space, such as a scene that appears to extend into the distance

pigment: fine powder that produces color; when mixed with oil or water, it becomes paint

primary color: any of a group of colors from which all other colors can be obtained by mixing

proportion: the appropriate relation of parts to each other or to the whole artwork

space: the feeling of depth in a work of art

studio: a space, room, or building in which an artist works

Key Words

art dealers: people who buy and sell art

avant-garde: art that is new and experimental for its time

caricatures: comical portraits that exaggerate the features of their subjects

contemporaries: people living at the same time as someone else

curators: people who look after the collections of an art gallery or museum

dappled: marked with spots

drafted: selected for military service

exhibition: a public display of the works of artists

Franco-Prussian War: a war between France and Prussia that took place from 1870 to 1871

Impressionism: an art movement originating in France in the 1800s that attempted to capture fleeting impressions of a subject rather than detailed realism

palettes: the ranges of colors used by an artist in making works of art

pastels: drawings done using crayons made from powdered pigments

silhouette: a dark shape against a light background

stationer: someone who sells stationery, such as paper and envelopes

synthetic: artificial

Index

Academy of Fine Arts 5, 12, 13, 24
Art Institute of Chicago 27

Barbizon school 11
Boudin, Eugène 8, 10, 20, 29
Boulevard des Capucines 18
brushwork 5, 11, 17, 30

Coquelicots [Poppy Field] 19

Doncieux, Camille 12, 20, 21, 22, 29
Durand-Ruel, Paul 22, 27, 29

Giverny 7, 21, 22, 24, 25, 29
Gleyre, Charles 9, 10, 13, 20

Hoschedé, Alice 21
Hoschedé, Blanche 24

Impression, Sunrise 13, 17, 21, 29
Impressionism 5, 21

Jongkind, Johan Barthold 10, 29

Lecadre, Marie-Jeanne 7, 9
Le Havre 6, 7, 12, 13
London 7, 20, 22, 27

Monet, Claude-Adolphe 6, 7, 8, 20
Monet, Louise-Justine Aubrée 6, 7, 20
Monet, Michel 24, 26
Musée Marmottan Monet 26

National Gallery 27

Paris 6, 7, 9, 10, 11, 16, 18, 19, 20, 22, 26, 29
Paris Salon 12, 13, 29
plein air 8, 10, 14, 15, 20, 29

Water Lilies 22, 29
Women in the Garden 16

Log on to www.av2books.com

AV² by Weigl brings you media enhanced books that support active learning. Go to www.av2books.com, and enter the special code found on page 2 of this book. You will gain access to enriched and enhanced content that supplements and complements this book. Content includes video, audio, weblinks, quizzes, a slide show, and activities.

AV² Online Navigation

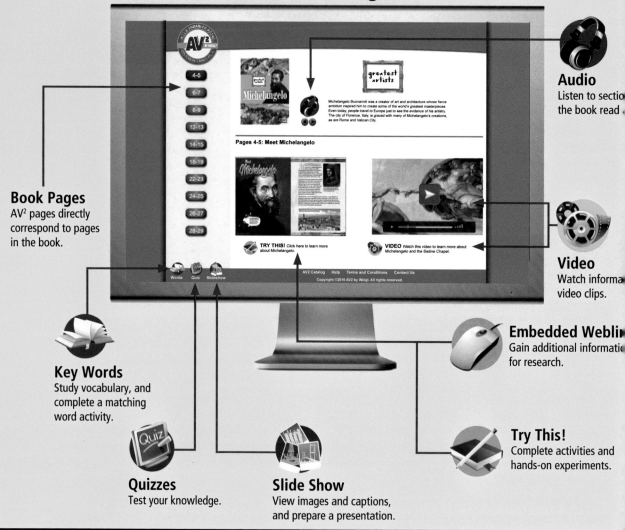

Audio
Listen to sectio the book read

Book Pages
AV² pages directly correspond to pages in the book.

Video
Watch informa video clips.

Key Words
Study vocabulary, and complete a matching word activity.

Embedded Weblir
Gain additional informatio for research.

Try This!
Complete activities and hands-on experiments.

Quizzes
Test your knowledge.

Slide Show
View images and captions, and prepare a presentation.

AV² was built to bridge the gap between print and digital. We encourage you to tell us what you like and what you want to see in the future.

Sign up to be an AV² Ambassador at www.av2books.com/ambassador.

Due to the dynamic nature of the Internet, some of the URLs and activities provided as part of AV² by Weigl may have changed or ceased to exist. AV² by Weigl accepts no responsibility for any such changes. All media enhanced books are regularly monitored to update addresses and sites in a timely manner. Contact AV² by Weigl at 1-866-649-3445 or av2books@weigl.com with any questions, comments, or feedback.